Contents

What Is a Whale?

Whales are very big **mammals** that live in the ocean. They are not fish. Like all mammals, whales are **warm-blooded**, breathe air, and feed their babies on mother's milk.

When whales come up for air, they breathe through **blowholes** on the tops of their heads.

blowholes

eye

tongue

There are many different kinds of whales. This book follows the journey of a gray whale.

tail flukes

A female gray whale can be 50 feet long when fully grown. That's longer than a bus. It can weigh up to 38.5 tons—as much as six or seven African elephants. Males are almost as big.

fin

What Is Migration?

Migration means going to live in a different place for part of the year. Many animals do this, but gray whales travel farther than most.

In the summer, gray whales live in the Arctic Ocean, where there is plenty of food for them.

6

In the fall, the Arctic Ocean becomes very cold. The whales swim south to warmer waters in the Pacific Ocean.

When spring comes, the whales return to the Arctic.

The maps on pages 28 and 29 show how far the gray whales swim.

What Do Whales Eat?

Some whales have teeth and can eat fish. The gray whale has no teeth. Instead, it has **baleen plates**. The plates look a lot like combs.

krill

baleen plates

The whale gulps sea water, which is full of tiny animals called **krill**. Then the whale squeezes the water out of its mouth. The krill is trapped by the baleen, and the whale swallows the krill.

Whales have huge mouths, but the krill they eat are very small. They float in the sea in large numbers.

8

In the Arctic Ocean in summer, there is plenty of krill to eat. The whales spend the long summer days feeding.

whale feeding on summer days

9

Why Do Whales Migrate?

Whales migrate to warm water to **mate** and give birth. When the weather in the Arctic gets colder, the whales start to swim toward warmer seas. Soon after they reach the warmer water, the male and female whales mate. Then the female whales become **pregnant**.

splashing tail

How do whales breathe?

Whales cannot breathe underwater. They have to come up to the surface to breathe air.

A whale's nostrils are on the top of its head. They are called blowholes. Gray whales have two blowholes.

When the whale breathes out, the **water vapor** in its breath turns into mist. This spray is called the whale's **blow**.

blow

blowholes

What Happens After Mating?

In the spring, the pregnant whale swims north again. She moves with a group of whales called a **pod**. Together they swim thousands of miles back to the cool **polar** oceans.

All this time, the baby whale is growing inside its mother.

Hold the page up
to the light to see
if you can see the
baby whale.

13

The baby whale grows inside its mother.

The growing baby will stay inside its mother for about a year until it is ready to be born.

Why Does the Mother Return to the North?

Although the Pacific Ocean is warmer than the Arctic Ocean, a mother whale will always return to the Arctic until she is ready to give birth. This is because there is much more food there—and she needs to eat lots of krill so that her baby will grow strong and healthy.

barnacles

When Is the Baby Whale Born?

When the weather becomes colder again, the whales start their journey to the south. When the mother reaches warmer waters, she finds a quiet place in which to give birth. The baby whale is called a **calf**. It is born tail-first.

adult female

The white patches on a gray whale's skin are groups of **barnacles**. These animals live on the whale but do not harm it. Soon the calf will have barnacles too.

calf

What Does the Calf Eat?

Whales are mammals, and all mammals feed their young mother's milk.

A newborn calf is around 15 feet long at birth—that's longer than most cars.

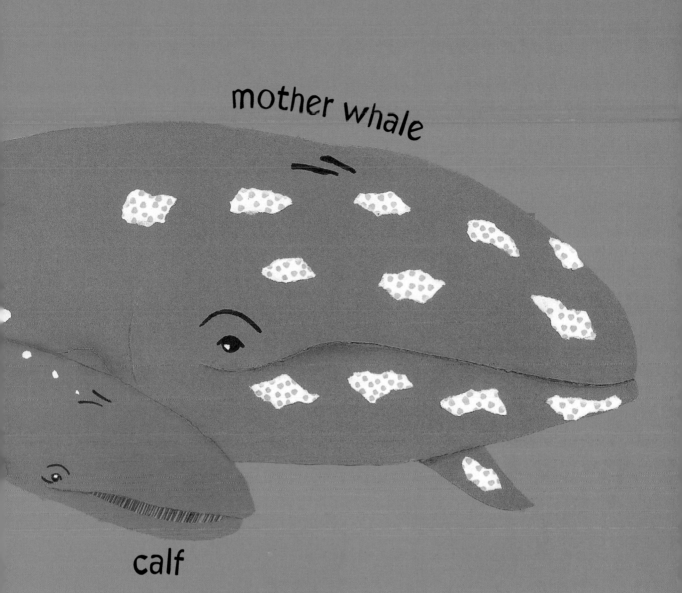

mother whale

calf

When spring comes, the mother and calf start to swim north again. It takes them many months to get back to the polar oceans. The calf must grow a thick layer of fat (called **blubber**) to keep it warm.

Do the Calf and Its Mother Stay Together?

Yes, the mother and calf make the journey back to the north together. By summertime, the whales and their young are home. They have finished their migration.

Of all the migrating whales, mothers and their calves will be the last to leave the warmer waters and head north.

mother and calf migrating north

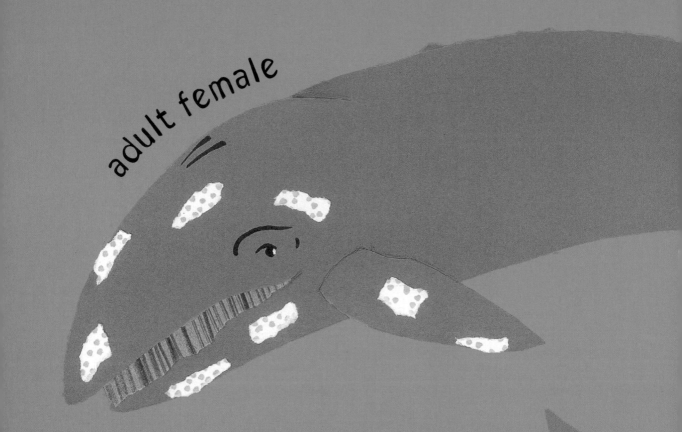

adult female

When Does the Calf Leave Its Mother?

When it is about seven months old, the calf stops drinking milk and begins to eat krill, just like an adult whale. At around one year of age, the calf leaves its mother.

Gray whales can live to be up to 60 years old.

young whale feeding on krill

23

How Long Is the Whales' Journey?

The gray whales' migration is one of the longest in the animal kingdom. In one year, a gray whale can travel up to 12,500 miles.

During its lifetime, a gray whale will travel a distance equal to flying to the moon and back!

whales and their young at home in the Arctic

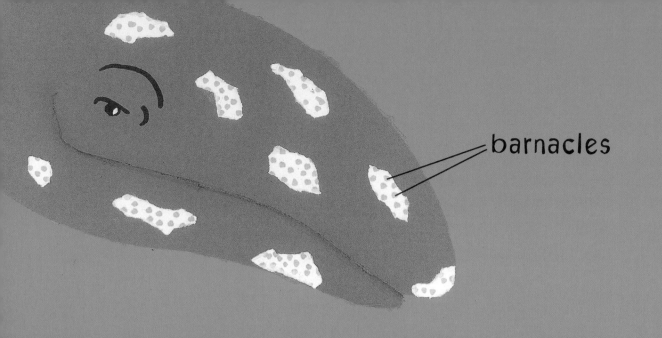

barnacles

Whale Facts

Gray whales may have as much as 440 pounds of barnacles clinging to their head and body.

Most gray whales roll onto their right side when they are feeding. Since the baleen plates on the right are used more, they wear down more quickly than those on the left side.

In some years, the whales migrate earlier or later than usual. This probably depends on the weather and on how much krill there is for the whales to eat.

A gray whale's cruising speed during migration is about 3 to 6 miles per hour.

There used to be gray whales in the Atlantic Ocean, but they died out there about 300 years ago. This may have been because people hunted too many of them.

Gray whales sleep on the surface, with their blowholes just above the water. When they are migrating, they do not sleep at all.

Gray whales are sometimes attacked by killer whales or sharks. When this happens, the mother whale will fight to protect her calf.

In 1997, a sick gray whale calf was found off the coast of California. Scientists at an amusement park nursed her back to health and returned her to the ocean a year later.

Migration Map

This map shows how far gray whales swim each year during their great migration. They swim all along the coast of North America, from Alaska to Mexico, and back again.

Where in the world do gray whales live?

Most gray whales live along the Pacific coast of North America. A few gray whales live on the other side of the Pacific Ocean, near Japan and Korea.

North Pole

North America

South America

South Pole

28

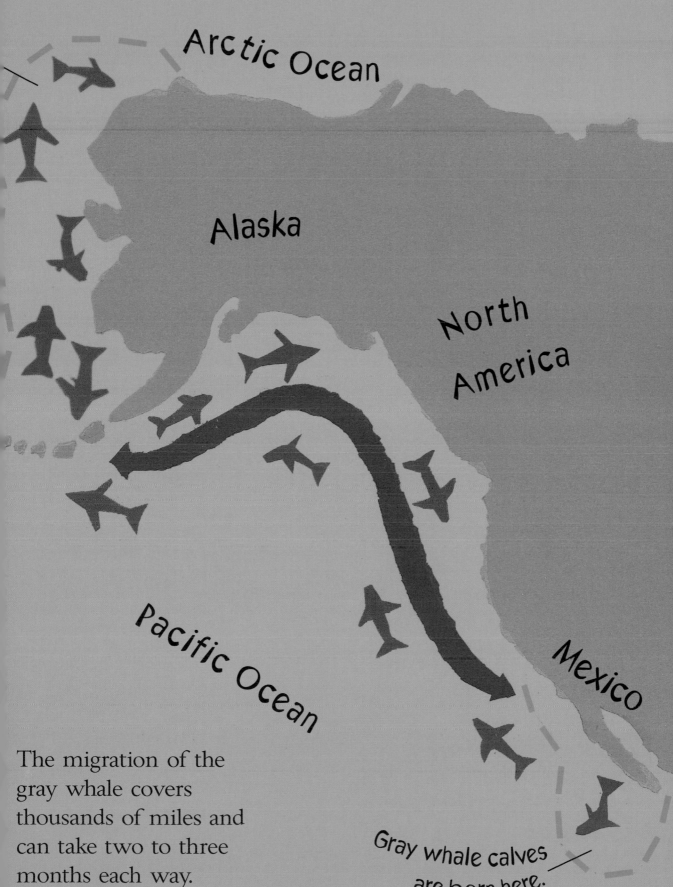

Arctic Ocean

Alaska

North America

Pacific Ocean

Mexico

The migration of the gray whale covers thousands of miles and can take two to three months each way.

Gray whale calves are born here.

The Life Cycle of a Gray Whale

adult whale

pregnant female

older calf eating krill

newborn calf with mother

Words to Remember

Baleen plates The bony plates in a gray whale's mouth that strain sea water for food.

Barnacle A small sea creature with a hard shell. It attaches itself to rocks, ships, and larger animals.

Blow A spray of water droplets from a whale's blowhole.

Blowholes The breathing holes on the top of a whale's head.

Blubber The layer of fat underneath a whale's skin.

Calf A young whale.

Flukes A whale's tail fins.

Krill Tiny shrimp-like animals that float in the sea.

Mammal A warm-blooded animal that breathes air, gives birth to live babies, and feeds them mother's milk.

Mating What happens when a male and a female animal join together to make a baby.

Migration Going to live in a different part of the world for part of the year.

Pod A family group of whales.

Polar Near the North or South Pole.

Pregnant Carrying a baby inside.

Warm-blooded Having a body temperature that stays the same all the time.

Water vapor Water that has changed from a liquid into an invisible gas.

Index

32